Bea and Jo
PRESS

Atlanta, GA

For Sahalae and Maya

Dedicated to Jordyn and Baleigh
...may you travel 'til
your hearts' content!

Picture It: India, 1959!
Dr. Martin Luther King, Jr. and his beloved wife, Coretta, globe-trotting across India! Just three years earlier, they'd led a successful bus boycott in Montgomery, Alabama. Wherever they went, the Kings were met with love and open arms! THIS is the story of their Fantastic, Incredible, Spectacular Adventure...

Grab your passports, let's GO!

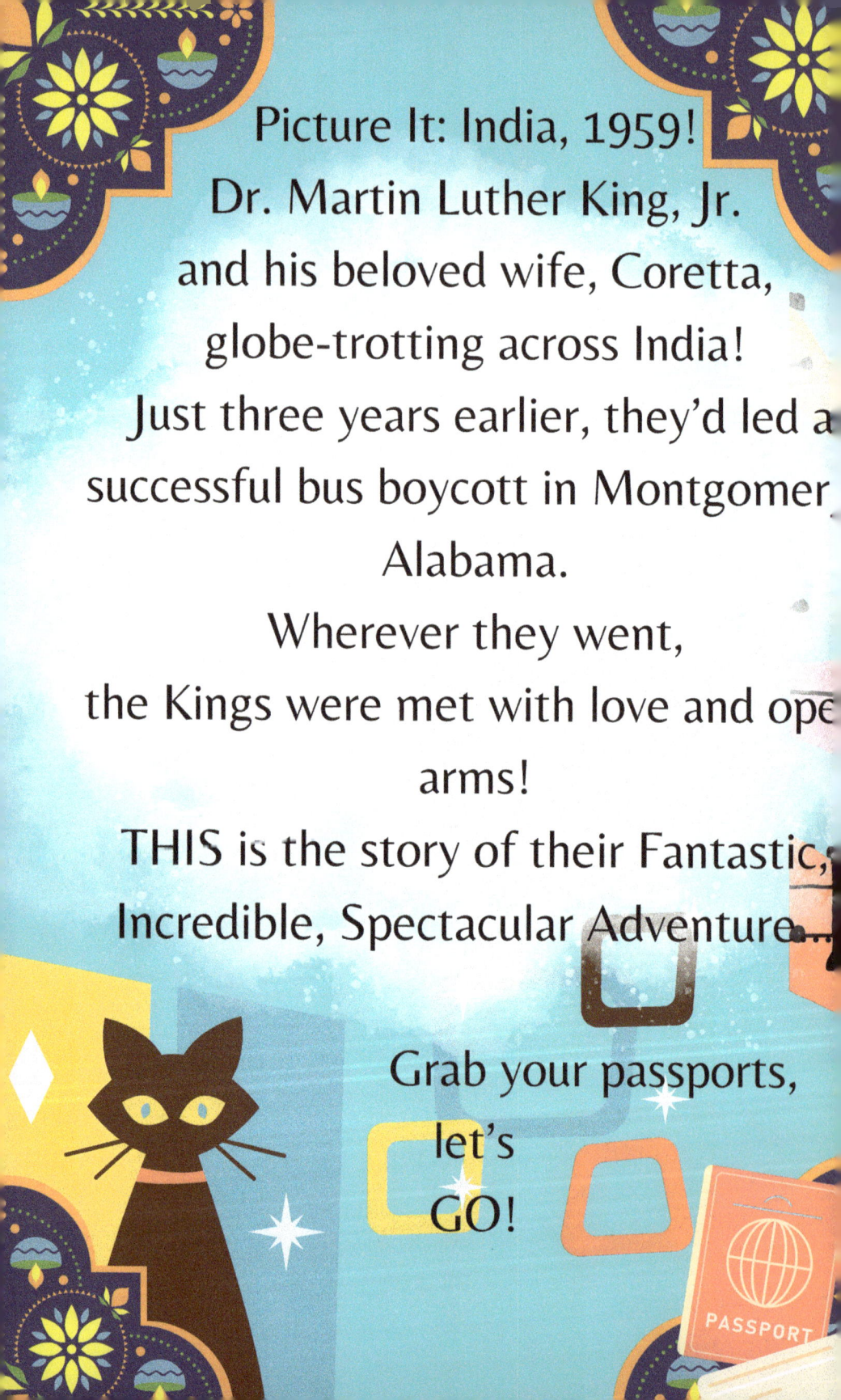

'To other countries I may go as tourist, but to India I come as a pilgrim.' - Dr. King

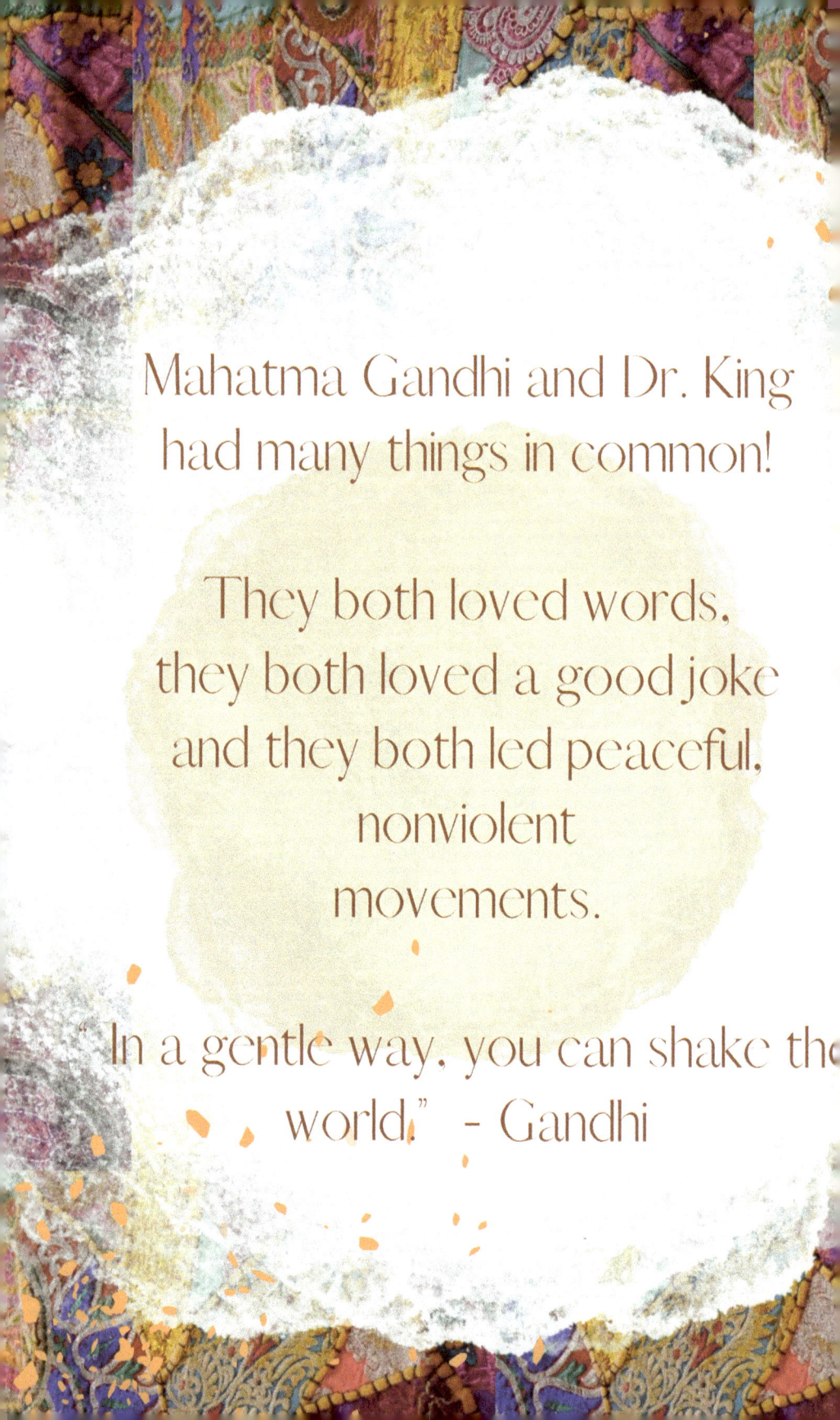

Mahatma Gandhi and Dr. King had many things in common!

They both loved words, they both loved a good joke and they both led peaceful, nonviolent movements.

"In a gentle way, you can shake the world." - Gandhi

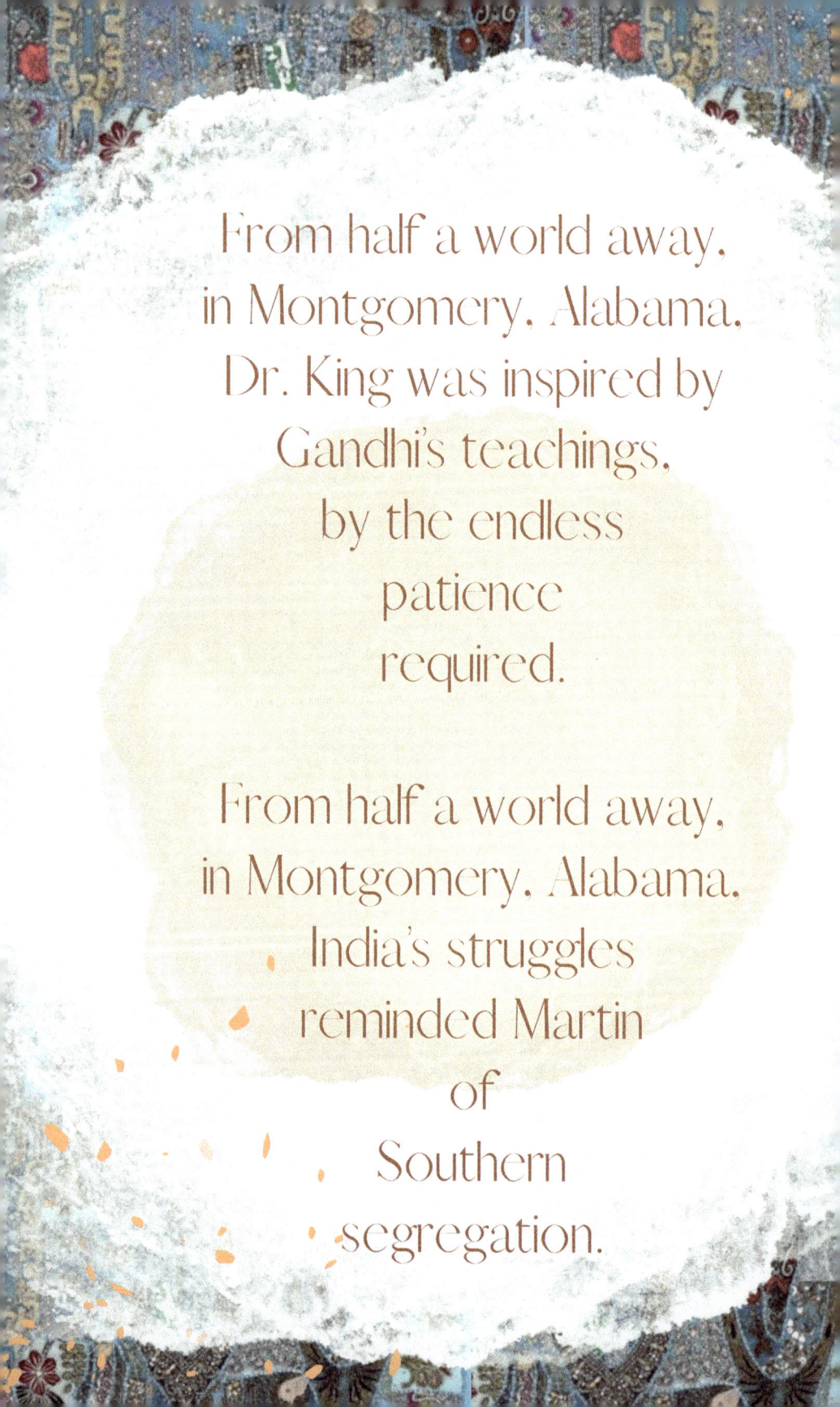

From half a world away,
in Montgomery, Alabama,
Dr. King was inspired by
Gandhi's teachings,
by the endless
patience
required.

From half a world away,
in Montgomery, Alabama,
India's struggles
reminded Martin
of
Southern
segregation.

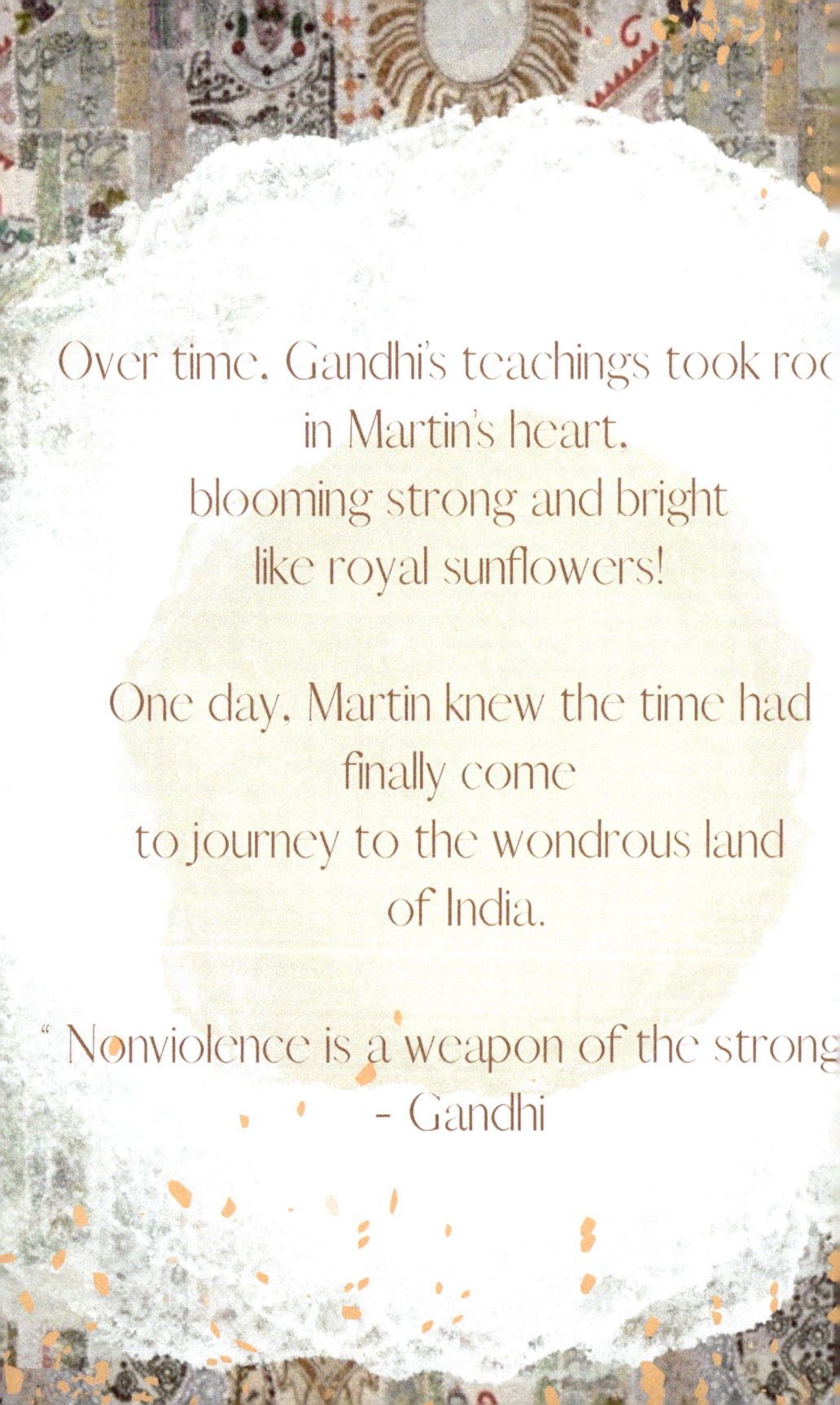

Over time, Gandhi's teachings took root
in Martin's heart,
blooming strong and bright
like royal sunflowers!

One day, Martin knew the time had
finally come
to journey to the wondrous land
of India.

" Nonviolence is a weapon of the strong
- Gandhi

Smiling wide like the morning sun,
airline tickets nestled in his
coat pocket,
young Martin and his dashing bride, Coret
board a sleek and handsome
jet!

Hearts filled with joy and excitement,
the couple walks hand in hand
carrying tidy, well-packed
luggage,
ready for an
international
ADVENTURE.

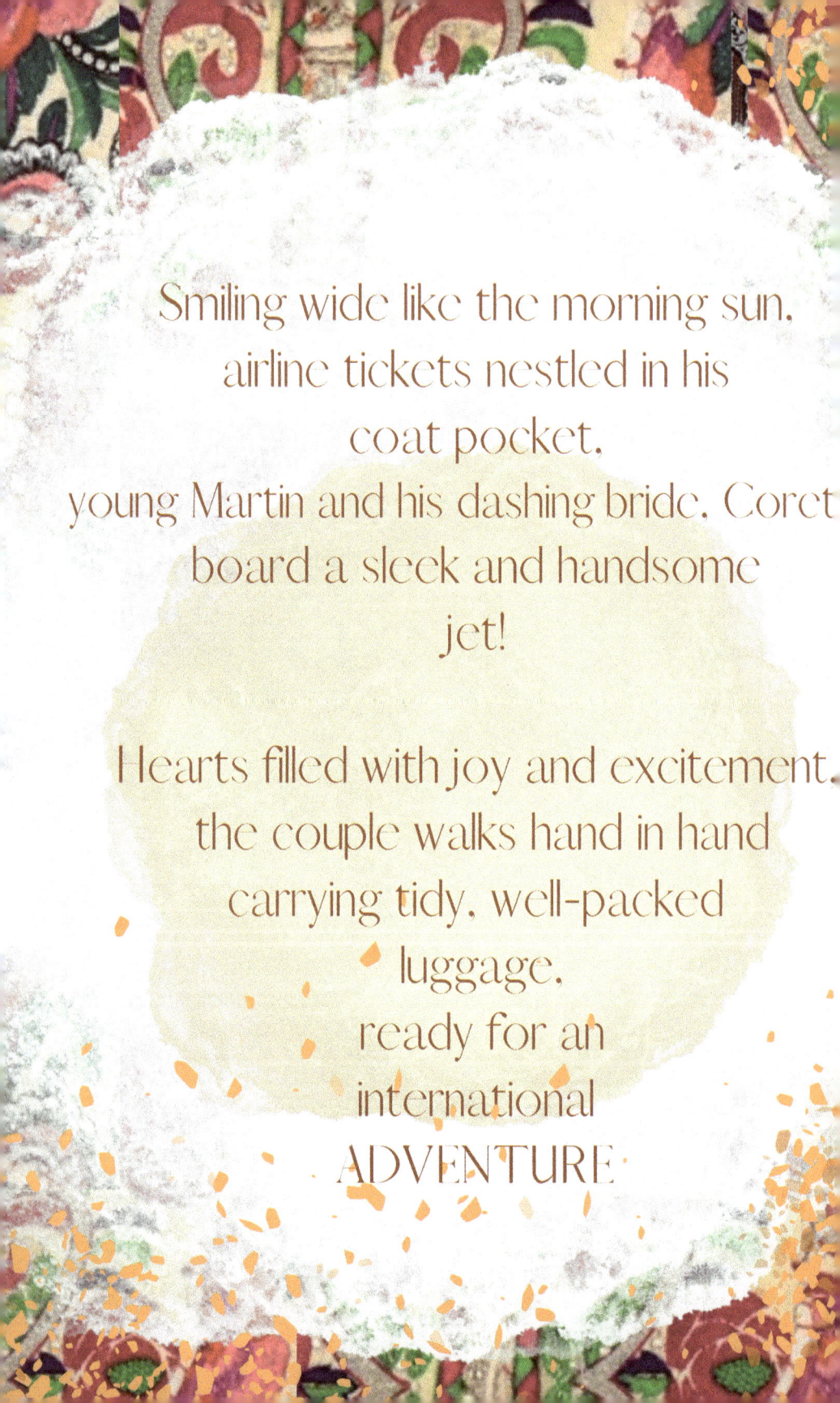

Soaring through glittery night skies,
gliding over rippling
ocean waves,
the morning sun peeks over the
horizon,
as they coast over Parisian cafes.

Hopscotching from Europe to Asia,
Martin and Coretta crisscross the
globe.
From the near, near West to the
far, far East,
India is a long, long way
from
Montgomery!

With passports in hand,
tidy luggage by their side,
the Kings safely land on
Indian soil.

Much to their delight,
they are greeted with cheers,
they are greeted with wide
open arms!

And much to their delight,
they are greeted with ENDLESS
forever
flower
bouquets.

"Learn as if you were to live forever."
—Gandhi

First stop?
The Taj Mahal,
majestic wonder of the world!
Hearts overflowing with gratitude,
Martin and Coretta are
amazed
by what they see:

Rows of columns stretching tall,
spiraling high and kissing the
clouds.
Glistening white marble, carved and
curved,
gleaming bright in the
brilliant
blue
sky.
A sweet silence drifts through the air,
one can barely hear a
sound.

Next Stop?
The Indian Embassy,
home of India's new democracy!
Prime Minister Nehru celebrates the Kings,
thanking them for their service and sacrifice.

President Nehru honors
the freedom fighters,
and together they make a vow
to forever continue the work
that Gandhi had just
begun.

" Where there is love there is life."
- Gandhi

First planes, now trains
...All Aboard!!

Seated sweetly side by side,
on a rambling passenger train,
winding, twisting through the
countryside,
from Patna to Gaya.

Scented spices perfume the air,
while Coretta's eyes delight
at the sunbursts of
brightly colored saris,
beautifully worn by
women and girls.

"The future depends on what we do in
the present." - Gandhi

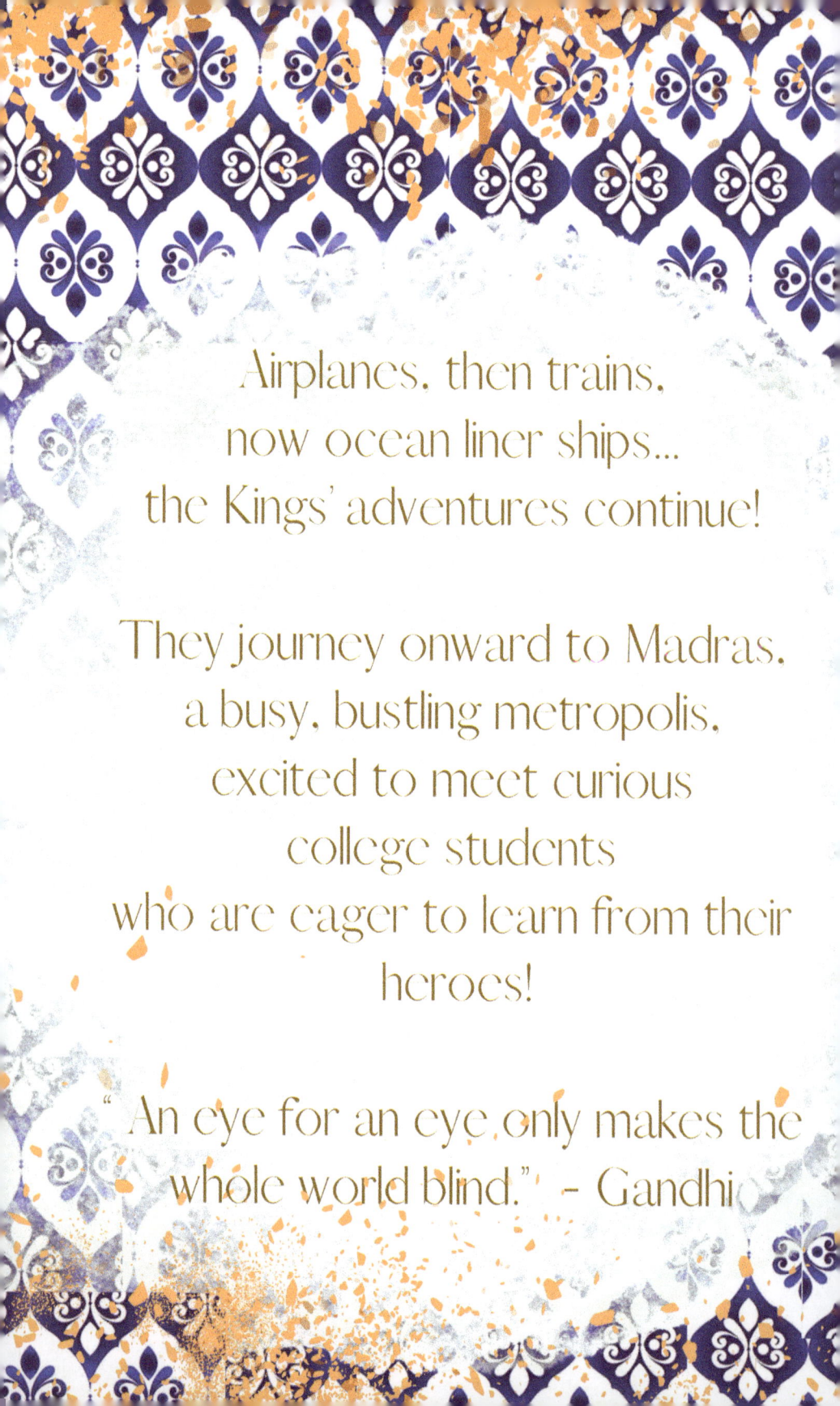

Airplanes, then trains,
now ocean liner ships...
the Kings' adventures continue!

They journey onward to Madras,
a busy, bustling metropolis,
excited to meet curious
college students
who are eager to learn from their
heroes!

"An eye for an eye only makes the
whole world blind." - Gandhi

Onward south to the tip of
Cape Camorin-
WIDE, GLORIOUS and GRAND,
swaddled by a bed of white
sea foam,
bathed in turquoise- blue cool
ocean waves.

The couple stands hand in hand,
their golden skin
warmed by the sun.
Legend has it that India began here
in this
most
beautiful
place.

The next morning
the Kings rise with the sun,
boarding an early-bird jet heading west!
They are off to the buzzing city of Mumbai,
the place where Gandhi called home.

Hand in hand, they enter Gandhi's house,
humbled to walk in his steps,
hearts overflowing with gratitude,
more determined to change
the WORLD!

"The best way to find yourself is to lose yourself in the service of others."
- Gandhi

As their travels slowly draw to an end,
the tireless couple has one final stop.
A dinner party is being held in their
honor,
in the lively capital of
New Delhi!

Martin and Coretta attend a glorious feast
filled with love, laughter and light-
a forever feast fit for royalty,
in honor of their final night.

Floating in flowy pinks and silks,
Coretta's sari sparkles and swirls!
A joyful evening of food and fellowship,
the time has come to bid India
FAREWELL

4 weeks, 12 days, 3 continents...
...planes, trains and boats!
The Kings return to Montgomery,
overjoyed to see their family and friends!

And WHEREVER Martin and Coretta
traveled,
for always and
forevermore,
India's newly planted seeds of hope
bloomed tall,
like
sunflowers
in their
hearts.

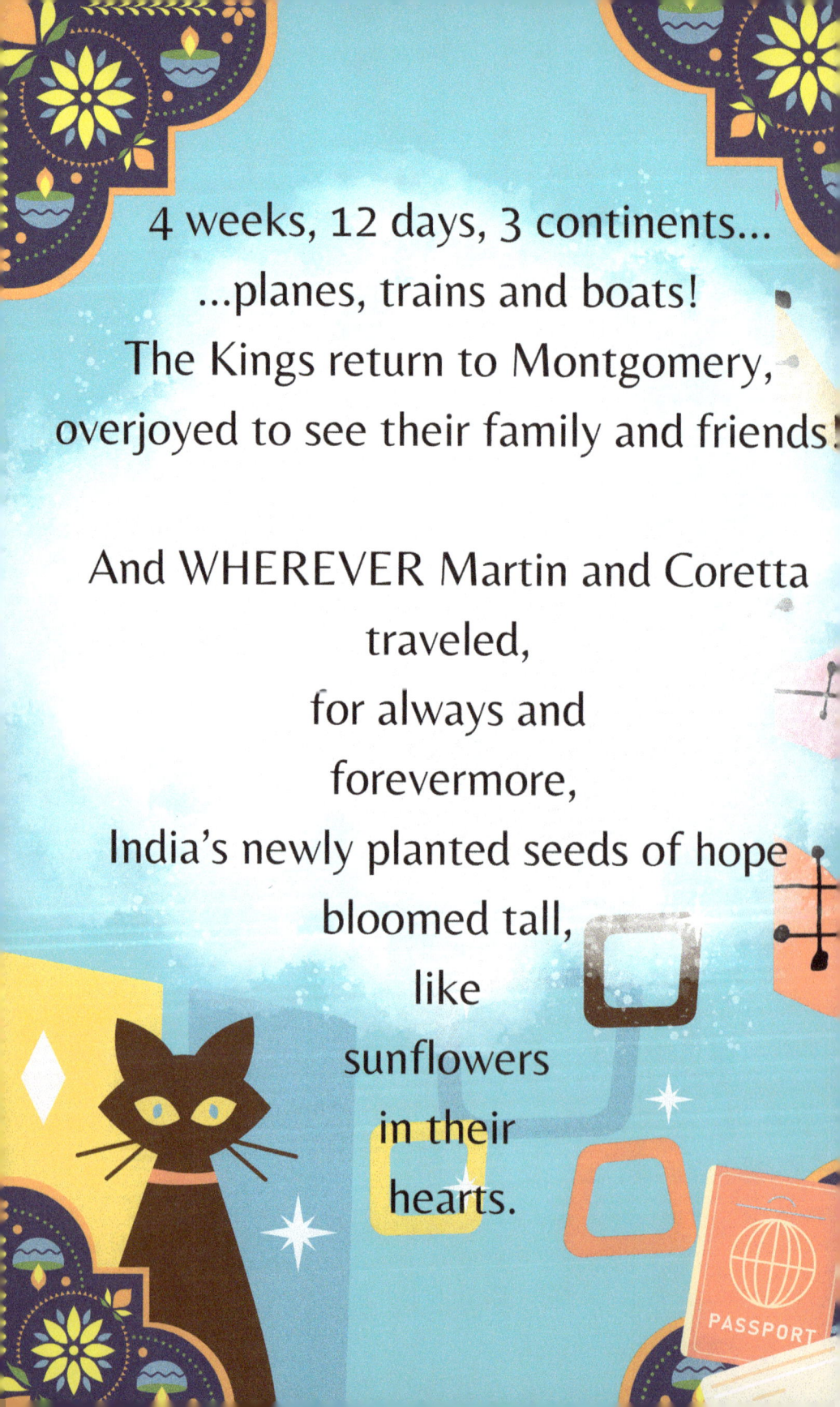

The End.

www.ingramcontent.com/pod-product-compliance
Lightning Source LLC
Chambersburg PA
CBHW050735010526
44107CB00010B/857